D0783484

Changing Seasons

Siân Smith

www.heinemannlibrary.co.uk
Visit our website to find out more information about Heinemann Library books.

To order:
Phone +44 (0) 1865 888066
Fax +44 (0) 1865 314091
Visit www.heinemannlibrary.co.uk

Heinemann Library is an imprint of Capstone Global Library Limited, a company incorporated in England and Wales having its registered office at 7 Pilgrim Street, London, EC4V 6LB – Registered company number: 6695582

First published in hardback in 2009

Edited by Rebecca Rissman, Charlotte Guillain and Siân Smith
Designed by Joanna Hinton-Malivoire
Picture research by Elizabeth Alexander and Sally Claxton
Production by Duncan Gilbert
Originated by Heinemann Library
Printed and bound in China by Leo Paper Group

ISBN 978 0 431 19390 8
13 12 11 10 09
10 9 8 7 6 5 4 3 2 1

British Library Cataloguing in Publication Data
Smith, Siân
Changing seasons. - (Acorn plus)
1. Seasons - Juvenile literature
I. Title
508.2

Acknowledgements

The author and publisher are grateful to the following for permission to reproduce copyright material: ©Alamy pp.**17 bottom left** (67Photo), **17 top right** (blickwinkel), **17 top left** (Imagestate), **21 right** (INSADCO Photography), **19 right** (John Cancalosi); ©Capstone Global Library Ltd. pp.**10 left**, **10 right, 11 left, 11 right** (Trevor Clifford); ©Corbis pp. **04 left** (Zefa/Roman Flury), **04 right** (Image100), **6 right** (Zefa/Parque), **7 right** (epa/Peter Foley), **12** (Mark Bolton),**16** (George McCarthy), **20 left** (Lynda Richardson), **21 left** (Scott Gibson); ©Digital Stock p.**18 top right**; ©Digital Vision p.**20 right** (Rob van Petten); ©Getty Images pp.**04 middle left** (Floria Werner), **7 left** (The Image Bank/Peter Lilja); ©iStockphoto pp.**5** (Bojan Tezak), **19 left** (Dutchy), **04 middle right** (Inga Ivanova); ©PhotoDisc. 1993 p. **22 middle left** (Photolink); ©PhotoDisc. 1997 p.**18 left** (Alan D Carey); ©PhotoDisc. 1997 p. **17 bottom right** (Jeremy Woodhouse); ©PhotoDisc. 1998 pp.**22 right**, **22 middle right** (Life File. Andrew Ward); ©Photodisc pp.**13 left** (Photolink), **13 bottom right** (Photolink F Schussler), **13 top right** (Photolink. Kent Knudson); ©Photolibrary pp.**8** (Robert Harding Travel/Pearl Bucknell), **6 left** (Roy Morsch); ©Punchstock pp.**14** (Digital Vision), **22 left** (Stockbyte); ©Shutterstock pp. **18 bottom right** (drKaczmar), **15** (Kokhanchikov), **9** (Suzanne Tucker).

Cover photographs of trees reproduced with permission of ©Shutterstock/ spring (Alexei Novikov)/ summer (Petr Jilek)/ autumn (Javarman)/ winter (Kokhanchikov). Back cover photograph reproduced with permission of ©PhotoDisc. 1997 (Alan D Carey).

Every effort has been made to contact copyright holders of any material reproduced in this book. Any omissions will be rectified in subsequent printings if notice is given to the publisher.

Contents

Some words are shown in bold, **like this.** They are explained in "Words to know" on page 23.

Different seasons

There are four seasons every year.
The four seasons follow a **pattern**.

The pattern is spring, summer, autumn, winter.
After winter it is spring again.

Weather

spring

summer

The weather changes in different seasons. In spring it can be warm and wet. In summer it can be hot and dry.

autumn

winter

In autumn it can be cool and foggy. Sometimes there are strong winds in autumn. In winter the weather can be very cold.

winter

The weather in different seasons can depend on where you live. Winter is always the coldest season, but not all places have snow in winter.

winter

What is winter like where you live? Does it always snow in winter where you live?

Clothes

We wear different clothes in different seasons to match the weather. In spring we need to wear clothes that keep us dry. In summer we need to wear clothes that keep us cool.

In autumn we need to wear clothes that keep us warm.
In winter we need to wear even warmer clothes.

Plants

spring

In spring lots of new plants start to grow. Trees and other plants grow new leaves. You might see lots of flowers in spring.

summer

In summer many plants grow fruit. Which summer fruits can you see in these pictures?

autumn

In autumn the leaves of some plants change colour. The leaves start falling to the ground. Some plants keep their leaves and stay green. What happens to plants during autumn where you live?

winter

In winter many trees have lost all of their leaves. It is hard for some plants to stay alive in winter. Some plants that die in winter leave **seeds** that will grow into new plants in spring.

Animals

winter

Some animals sleep all winter. This is called **hibernation**. Hedgehogs, tortoises, bears, snakes, and some mice all hibernate in winter.

spring

Animals that have been asleep through the winter wake up in spring. In spring lots of animals have babies. Which baby animals can you see here?

summer

In the summer lots of insects are busy collecting food. You might see ladybirds looking for food. You might see bees and butterflies on flowers.

autumn

In autumn lots of animals collect food for the winter. Some animals eat a lot in autumn so that they can **hibernate** in winter. Some birds and fish move to places where the weather is warmer.

Things we do

spring

summer

In spring some people like to work in their gardens and plant things. In summer people like to play outside. Lots of people go on **holiday** in the summer.

autumn

winter

In autumn some people like to make **bonfires** and watch **fireworks**. You might see people sweeping up leaves in autumn. In winter many people like to feed hungry birds.

Guess the season

a

b

c

Which season does each picture show?

Answers on p. 23

Words to know

bonfire	outdoor fire. People sometimes burn dead branches and leaves on bonfires.
evergreen	an evergreen plant does not lose its leaves in the winter
firework	something that burns to make light and noise; fireworks are often seen high in the sky.
hibernation	sleeping or resting through the winter
holiday	break from work or school
pattern	happening in the same order
seed	plants make seeds. Seeds grow into new plants.

Answers to Guess the season

a = autumn b = spring c = winter d = summer

Index

Notes for parents and teachers

Before reading

Ask the children if they can tell you the names of the four seasons. Play a guessing game. Explain that you are going to give them some clues and they should try and suggest the appropriate season. For example: I am wearing a woolly scarf; I have a new t-shirt on; I like kicking the fallen leaves; there is blossom on the trees; it is very hot; daffodils are out in the park.

After reading

- You will need four cards. Draw a tree at a different season on each card – bare in winter, blossom in spring, green leaves in summer, and leaves falling down for the autumn. Shuffle the cards and hold up a card. The children have to tell you the season and something about that season, for example: there is snow in winter; there are lambs in spring; in summer it is hot.
- Make photocopies of the cards and give out one to each child. Tell the children they are to move around and look at each other's cards. They must make a "set" of cards (spring, summer, autumn, winter) with one card for each season and when they have made a set they must sit down.